Scooter
Challenges the Day

A True Story as told by Patrick Trotter

By Marielle D. Marne

Illustrated by Herb James

Print information available on the last page

To order additional copies of this book, contact:
Xlibris
1-888-795-4274
www.Xlibris.com
Orders@Xlibris.com

Rev. date: 03/12/2019

Scooter doesn't think he's a hero. He doesn't think he's a dog with special needs either. He thinks he's just like any other Jack Russell terrier. Scooter was born one October afternoon. His mother, JoJo, had Scooter and two other puppies.

While his brother and sister had four straight legs each, Scooter's front paw was crookedly bent inward. But, he played just like any other pup.

As all babies do, Scooter and his littermates grew until one day it was time for them to find new homes. Someone special had been watching over JoJo and her puppies as they grew. JoJo's owner had noticed him watching, too.

"Patrick," Miss Karen began, "we've noticed how much you seem to like JoJo and her children and wondered if you'd like to have one? Two already have homes, but we are looking for a really good home for the last puppy."

"You see," she said, "he has a deformed little leg and he needs lots of love and attention so that he never feels left out or different from the other dogs." Patrick knew this was his lucky day and could not hide his excitement when he said, "Yes, I'd love to have this little dog."

It was no surprise that the tiny pup was scared. He was leaving his mother and the home where he grew up. He would no longer get to romp with his brother and his sister.

But as he snuggled into the arms of the man who held him, he knew he would be fine.

In his new home, Scooter settled right in. Patrick watched him do all the things puppies do. That included some barking. And some chewing. And some chasing. And more barking.

Patrick thought he might call his new companion Napoleon after the French General Bonaparte whose arm bent the same way as the puppy's paw did. When he saw him scoot around on the floor, much like a kid on a scooter, Patrick decided Scooter was the perfect name.

The years went by and Patrick and Scooter were never apart. Scooter loved to ride in Patrick's truck, so Patrick took him wherever he went.

When Scooter was at home, he was always by Patrick's side. He was either on the sofa cushion next to him or on his feet at the bottom of the bed. Scooter was thankful he had such a wonderful owner. Then one day, Scooter got the chance to show Patrick just how much his person meant to him.

Outside doing chores, Patrick started to sit down on an overturned bucket in the yard. Scooter jumped up on his leg and pushed him back really hard! Patrick almost lost his balance.

Not sure what was going on, Patrick was about to scold his pet for being so rough. Before he could even open is mouth, Scooter started barking and growling – not acting at all as he normally did.

Suddenly, Patrick saw a four-foot rattlesnake! It would have bitten him had Scooter not jumped between them. Knowing he was safe, Patrick was about to call Scooter away from the venomous snake but Scooter had other ideas. Barking and growling, Scooter was not about to give the snake a chance to hurt his beloved master.

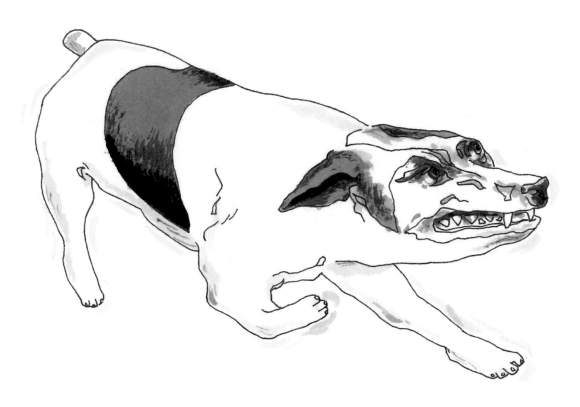

Sensing he was in trouble as well, the snake tried to protect himself by biting Scooter.

The fifteen-pound dog with the misshapen front paw would not give up, so the snake bit him again. And again. And again, for ten bites in the head and neck. Patrick kept yelling for Scooter to get away from the snake, but the daring dog didn't listen. Soon, the snake's poison started working on Scooter. He started to stumble and sway. The snake was super scared and slithered away.

Patrick grabbed Scooter in his arms. He remembered the first time he brought his furry friend home as a puppy cradled in his arms as he was now. He was worried Scooter might not be able to live with the poison going through his little body.

Patrick sprinted to the truck and sped to the veterinary office. He pleaded with Scooter to hang in there. Patrick knew had it not been for Scooter, he might have been bitten by the rattlesnake instead. Patrick cried as he drove. He thought how lonely it would be without his four-legged companion and he drove even faster.

"Quick!" Patrick yelled as he ran through the double doors at the vet's, "My dog got bitten by a rattlesnake. He needs help!"

Doctor Cliff Faver took Scooter from Patrick and took him to the back room where emergencies were handled. He had to give him three shots of medicine so the snake's venom wouldn't hurt Scooter anymore.

Slowly, Scooter showed signs the medicine was working. The vet let the swollen patient rest and went back out front to find out what had happened. As Patrick told everyone in the office how Scooter had protected him, they all said what a brave terrier he was. Especially since he had a deformed front foot.

Scooter could hear everyone talking about him and calling him a hero. He thought to himself that he just did what any other dog would do. He wondered what all the talk was about his foot. It never seemed to slow him down.

Matter of fact, he thought, just last week I would have caught that rascally rabbit in the yard had it not gotten through the fence.

Scooter knows nothing can get you down if you don't let it. He knows that the bunny that escaped through the fence had nothing to do with the fact Scooter runs on three legs. It was the fence that let that happen.

He also knows you do things for the people you love because it's the only right thing to do. Scooter didn't think he was going to get hurt in the rattlesnake fight, but he was glad it was him and not Patrick who got bitten. But, they look out for each other!

So now you know why Scooter doesn't think he's a hero. And, he's surely not handicapped in his eyes. Maybe differently-abled is a better way to look at it.

Whatever you call it, he's just a faithful little dog who wanted to thank his guardian for all he's been given.

AFTERWORD

I'm happy to have been able to share the story of Scooter and his heroism with readers of all ages. He was a remarkable little dog who was much loved by Patrick. Scooter deserved all the recognition he received for his altruistic feat of keeping Patrick safe from the everyday dangers that lurk in Arizona's Sonoran Desert.

This true tale could not have been told without the help of Patrick Trotter on Scooter's behalf. And, it would not have had a happy ending without the expertise of Dr. Cliff Faver at Animal Health Services. I am thankful to fellow author and friend, Jim Raymond, for getting Herb James (may he RIP) involved in the illustrations. That had been a stumbling block for a stick-figure drawer like myself. Of course, to my family and friends who had to endure the long process it took to see this book to publication, I am forever grateful for your enthusiasm, love and support.

Printed in the United States
By Bookmasters